Vowel Digraphs

by Claire Daniel

SCHOLASTIC
PROFESSIONAL BOOKS

NEW YORK • TORONTO • LONDON • AUCKLAND • SYDNEY

Dear Teacher,

Nothing can be more important in the primary grades than instilling in children the joy of reading and teaching them the skills to become successful, lifelong readers. To do this, we must teach children how to unlock the mysteries of print. Reading instruction that includes systematic and explicit phonics instruction is essential to achieve this goal.

Phonics instruction unlocks the door to understanding sounds and the letters or spelling patterns that represent them. Quality phonics instruction engages children, provides opportunities for them to think about how words work, and offers reading and writing experiences for children to apply their developing skills. The playful, purposeful activities in the *Fun With Phonics!* series offer practice, reinforcement, and assessment of phonics skills. In combination with your daily reading instruction, these activities will help to capture the fun and excitement associated with learning to read.

Enjoy!

Wiley B.

Wiley Blevins, Reading Specialist

Scholastic Inc. grants teachers permission to photocopy the reproducible pages from this book for classroom use. No other parts of this publication may be reproduced in whole or in part, or stored in a retrieval system, or transmitted in any form by any means, electronic, mechanical, photocopying, recording or otherwise, without permission of the publisher. For information regarding permission, write to Scholastic Professional Books, 555 Broadway, New York, NY 10012-3999.

Cover Design: Vincent Ceci, Liza Charlesworth, and Jaime Lucero
Cover Illustration: Abby Carter
Interior Illustrations: Rick Brown

Series Development by Brown Publishing Network, Inc.
Editorial: Elinor Chamas
Interior Design and Production: Diana Maloney and Kathy Meisl

Copyright © 1997 by Scholastic Inc. All rights reserved.
ISBN 0-590-76496-9
Printed in the U.S.A.

Contents

Using "Fun with Phonics!"	4
Family Letter	5
Poem *Good Afternoon*	6
Gently Down the Stream *Digraphs ee, ea*	7
Crossword Puzzle *Long e Spelled e, ea, ee*	8
Riddle in the Middle *Digraphs ai, ay*	9
Use Those Clues! *Digraphs ie, oe*	10
Where Did the Ball Go? *Reviewing ie, oe, ee, ea, ai, ay*	11
Picture This! *Long o Spelled o, ow*	12
Finish the Rhymes *Digraph oa*	13
Round and Round *Long e Spelled y, ey*	14
Puzzle Rhymes *Digraph oo*	15
Word Search *Digraph oo*	16
Concentration *Digraph ea*	17
The Crawling Baby *Digraph aw*	18
Find the Treasure *Reviewing Vowel Digraphs*	19
Show What You Know *Standardized Test-Taking Skills*	20
Take-Home Book *A Book of Riddles*	21–22
Classroom Fun *Group Games and Activities*	23–25
Instant Activities *More Ideas for Quick and Easy Practice*	26–27
Story Shapes Patterns	28
Word Bank	29
Teacher Notes	29
Word/Picture Card Set	30–31
Observation Checklist	32

Using "Fun With Phonics"

Fun With Phonics! is a set of hands-on activity resource books that make phonics instruction easy and fun for you and the children in your classroom. Following are some ideas to help you get the most out of *Fun With Phonics!*

Classroom Management

Reproducibles Reproducible pages 7–19 offer a variety of individual and partner activities. Simple directions to the children are augmented when necessary by *Answers or Game Directions* in the *Teacher Notes* section on page 29.

Directions You may wish to go over the directions with children and verify that they can identify all picture cues and read any words in the activities before they begin independent work.

Games When children play partner games, you may want to circulate in order to make sure children understand procedures.

Working with the Poem

A poem on page 6 introduces the phonics element in this book, vowel digraphs. Read this page aloud to children. Duplicate the poem so that children can work with it in a variety of ways:

Personal Response Read the poem aloud and have children talk about it.

Phonemic Awareness Have children listen for a particular vowel sound as you read the poem aloud.

Sound to Letter Write the poem on chart paper, and have children circle words with vowel digraphs.

Dramatization Encourage groups of three children to perform the poem, with one taking the role of the sun, one taking the role of the moon, and one reading the narration in between.

Connecting School and Home

The Family Letter on page 5 can be sent home to encourage families to reinforce what children are learning. Children will also enjoy sharing the Take-Home Book on pages 21–22. You can cut and fold these booklets ahead of time, or invite children to participate in the process. You may also mount the pages on heavier stock and place the Take-Home Book in your classroom library.

Word/Picture Card Sets

Pages 30–31 of this book contain matching sets of Word/Picture Cards drawn from the vocabulary presented in this book. You may wish to mount these on heavier stock as a classroom resource. You may also wish to duplicate and distribute them to children for use in matching and sorting activities. Each child can use a large envelope to store the cards. Each title in the *Fun With Phonics!* series contains a new set of thirty-two Word/Picture Cards.

Assessment

Page 20, Show What You Know, provides children with targeted practice in standardized test-taking skills, using the content presented in this book in the assessment items. The Observation Checklist on page 32 gives you an informal assessment tool for monitoring the progress of individual children in your class.

Dear Family,

Your child is learning in school about vowel digraphs.

In a vowel digraph, two vowel letters together stand for one vowel sound. Some vowel digraphs are **ai, ea, oo, ie,** and **oa**.

tr**ai**n b**oa**t t**ie**

You may enjoy sharing some or all of the following activities with your child:

Rhyme a Word
Ask your child to play a rhyming game. Say a word such as *mail, day, bean, feed, tie, goat,* or *book* and ask children to say as many rhyming words as he or she can think of.

Comic Book Search
Use the comics section of the newspaper or a comic book to look for words with these vowel pairs: *ai, ay, ea, ee,* and *oa*. Circle each word. Then read the comics together.

Reading Together
To practice reading words with vowel digraphs, look through your child's Take-Home Book, "A Book of Riddles." Ask your child to underline words with vowel digraphs and to read the words for you.

You may also wish to look for these books in your local library:

Sincerely,

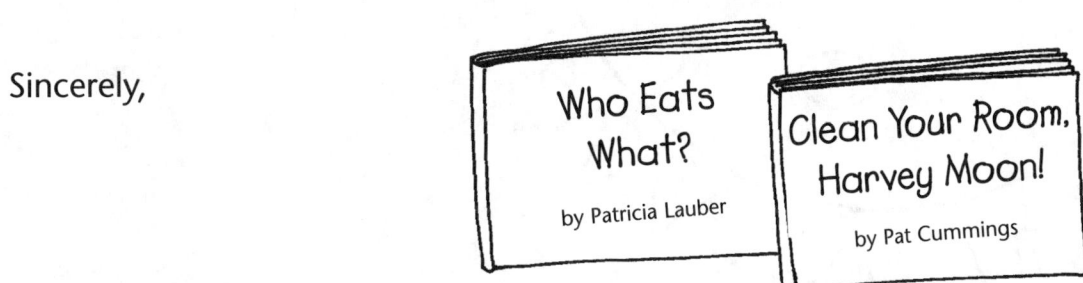

Who Eats What?
by Patricia Lauber

Clean Your Room, Harvey Moon!
by Pat Cummings

Vowel Digraphs

Name _____

Good Afternoon

"Good afternoon,"
Said the sun to the moon.
"I feel weak and could use a break."
Said the moon with a yawn,
"I can stay until dawn.
You sleep, and I'll keep awake!"

Name _____

Gently Down the Stream

Follow Jean down the stream. Color all the pictures whose long **e** names are in the box. Then answer the question at the bottom of the page.

jeans	bee	wheel	jeep
meal	tree	sheep	stream

What will Jean do?

Jean will eat the m ____ ____ l.

Digraphs ee, ea

Name _____

Crossword Puzzle

Look at each picture clue. Read the words in the box. Write each picture name in the puzzle.

| sheep | leaf | steam |
| wheel | jeep | jeans |

Across

2.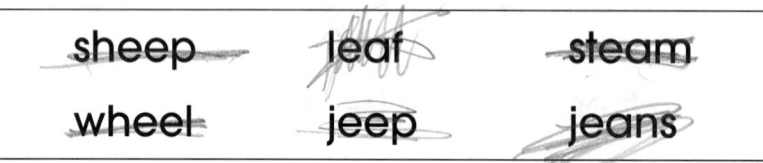
4.
5.

Down

1.
3.
4.

Digraphs **ea, ee**

Name _____

Riddle in the Middle

What falls but never gets broken?

Find the name of each picture in the word box. Write the word on the lines. Put one letter on each line. Now find the answer to the riddle. Read the letters in the tall box from top to bottom. Write the answer.

| pail | clay | chain | tray |

 1. T r a y

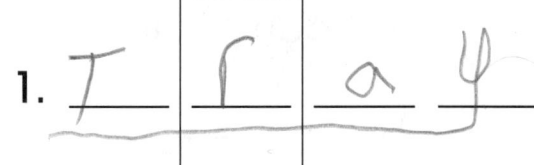

2. c l a y

 3. P a i l

 4. c h a i n

Answer: Rain .

Digraphs **ai, ay**

Name _____

Use Those Clues!

Read each clue. Draw a line to the picture that matches it. Write the word.

1. It is on your foot.

    It is a _____.

pie

2. A man can put it on.

    It is a _____.

hoe

3. You can eat this.

    It is a _____.

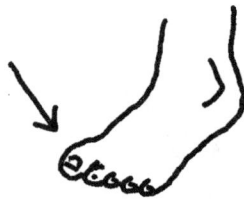
toe

4. You can dig with this.

    It is a _____.

tie

Name _____

Where Did the Ball Go?

The soccer team is looking for its ball. You can find it in the picture. Color shapes with long **e** words blue. Color shapes with long **i** and long **o** words red. Color shapes with long **a** words yellow.

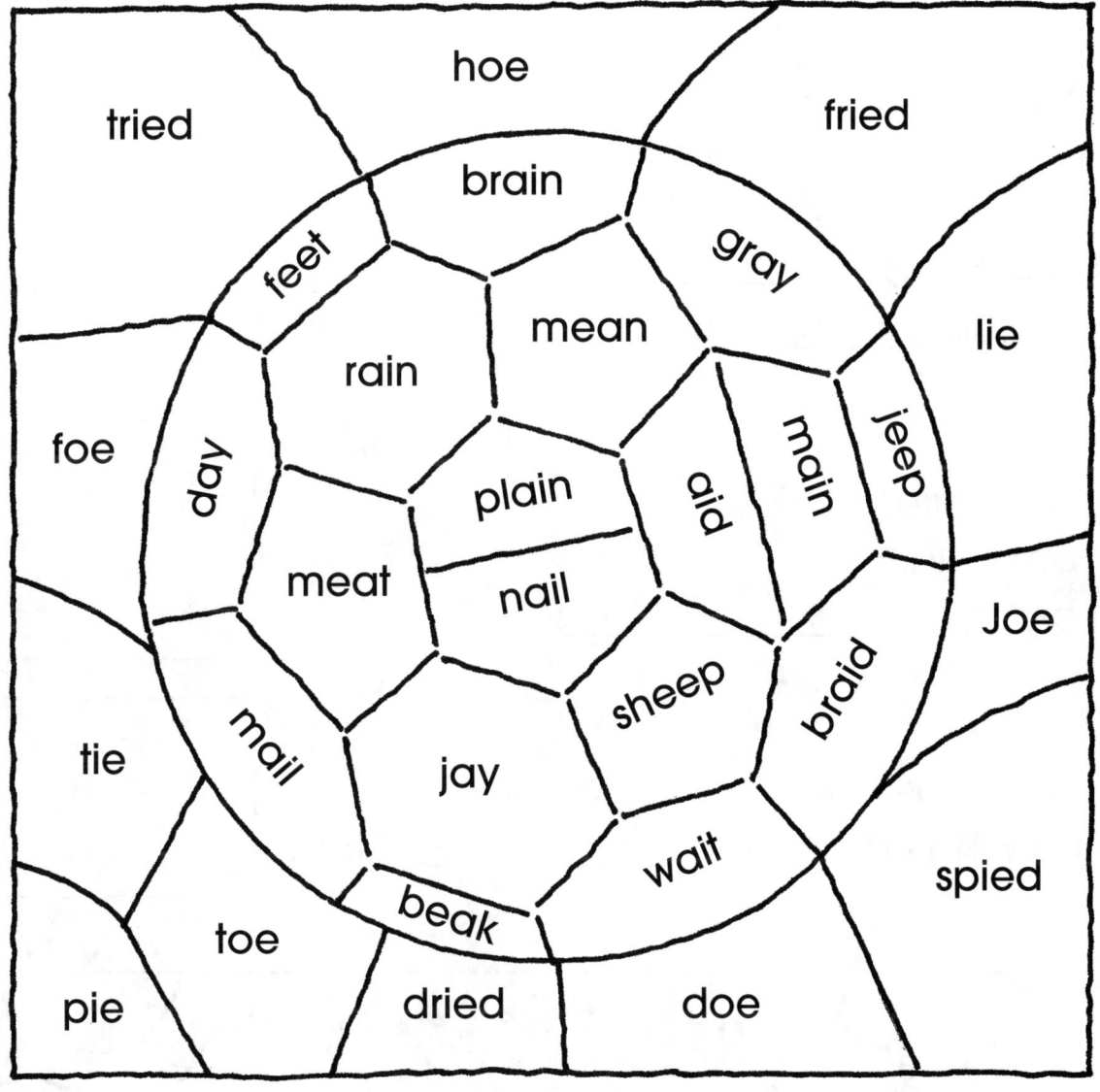

Reviewing **ie, oe, ee, ea, ai, ay**

Name _____

Picture This!

Read each riddle. Look at the pictures. Then cut and paste the picture that goes with each riddle. Write the word that completes each riddle. Use words from the box.

| go | snow | blow | elbow |

1. I am green.
   I tell you to _____.

2. I can bend.
   I am an _____.

3. I am white.
   I am cold.
   I am _____.

4. A boy does this.
   The wind can _____, too.

   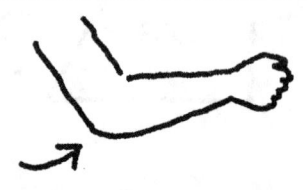

Long o Spelled o, ow

Name _____

Finish the Rhymes

Look at each picture. Then write the missing words to finish each rhyme. Use the words in the box.

| float | coat | road | boat | toad | goat |

1. The __toad__
   Sat by the __road__.

2. Joan puts a __coat__
   On her baby __goat__.

3. Our little __boat__
   Will not __float__!

Digraph **oa**

Name _____

Round and Round

Look at the scene. Color the things that are hiding. Their long **e** names are in the box. Then answer the question at the bottom of the page. Use a word from the box.

cherry	baby	bunny	puppy
monkey	key	daisy	penny

What pet can unlock a door?

A _____ !

Long e Spelled **y, ey**

Name _____

Puzzle Rhymes

Look at each puzzle picture at the top of the page. Look for a puzzle picture with a name that rhymes at the bottom of the page. Cut and paste each puzzle piece to make a puzzle rhyme.

POOL

BOOK

MOON

BOOT

HOOK

SCHOOL

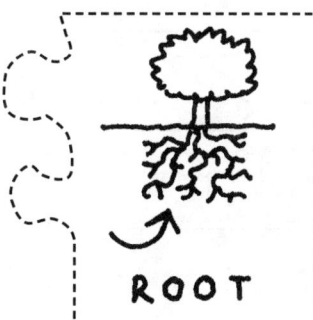
ROOT

SPOON

Digraph oo   15

Name _____

Word Search

In this puzzle, find 4 more words that rhyme with 📖.
Find 3 words that rhyme with 👤. Circle the words.
Then write the words on the lines.

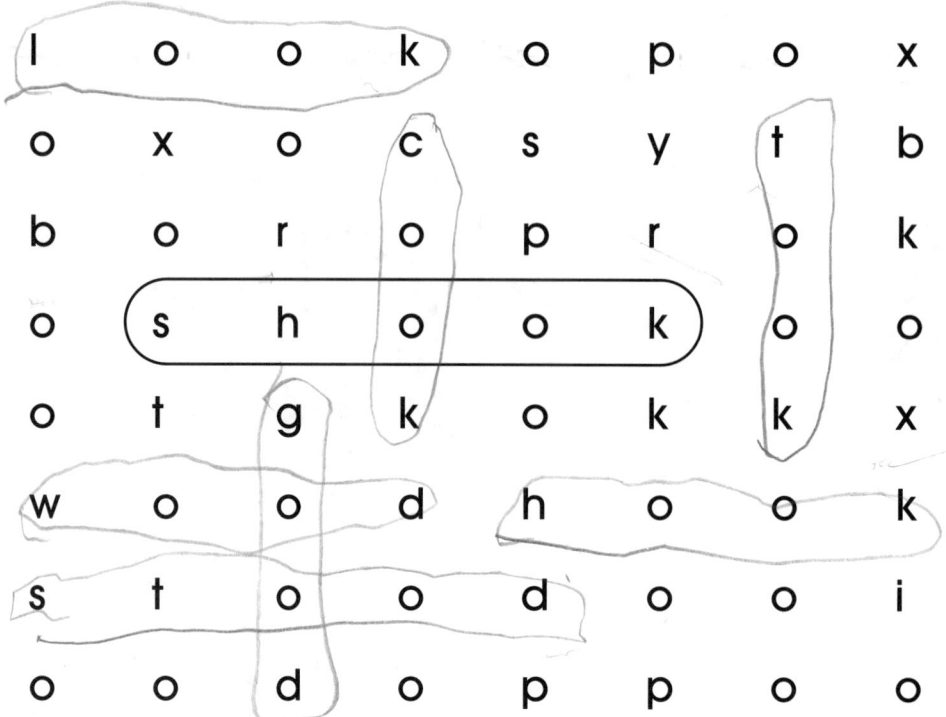

book

took
book
Look
Cook

hood

Stood
Wood
good

Name _____

Concentration

Cut out all the cards with a partner. Then play Concentration. Your teacher will tell you how to play the game.

 leaf	 steak	 break
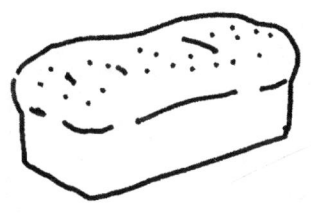 bread	 sweater	 head
 thread	 feather	 peach
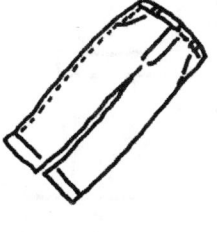 jeans	 seal	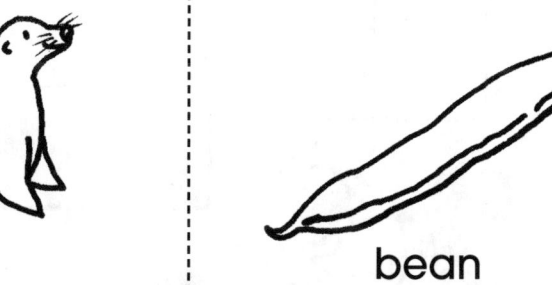 bean

Digraph **ea** 17

Name _____

The Crawling Baby

Help the baby crawl to its mother. Follow the pictures on the path whose **aw** names are in the box. Draw a path for the baby.

| yawn | paw | fawn | saw |
| shawl | straw | draw | claw |

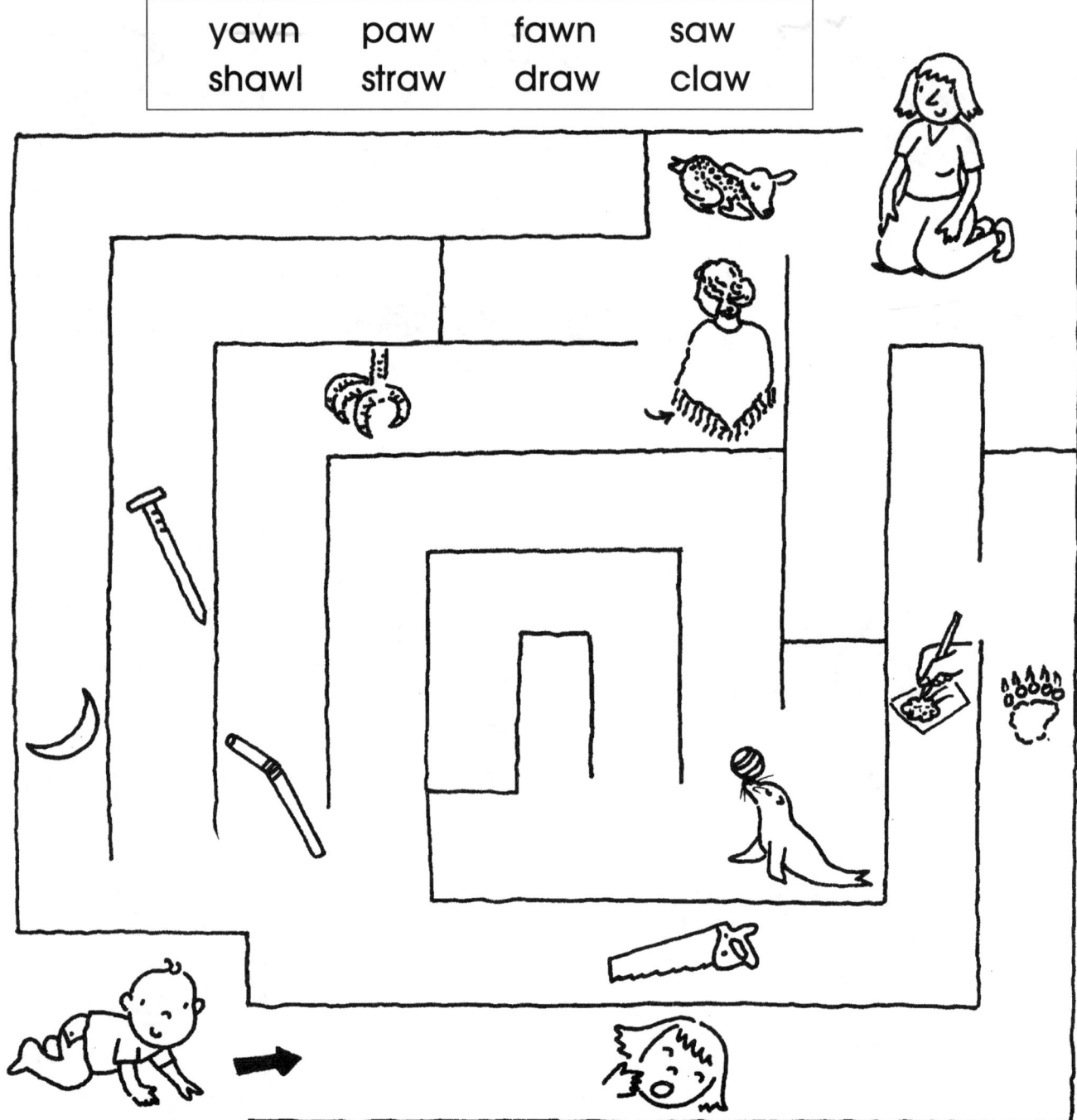

Words with **aw**

Name _____

Find the Treasure

Play this game with a partner. Who will get to the treasure first? Your teacher will tell you how to play.

Reviewing Vowel Digraphs

Name _____

Show What You Know

Look at the picture that begins each row. Fill in the circle next to the word that matches the picture.

1. ○ jacks ○ jeans ○ gate
2. ○ bell ○ boot ○ ball
3. ○ sheep ○ green ○ book
4. ○ wheel ○ hook ○ book
5. ○ well ○ clock ○ nail
6. ○ steak ○ sweater ○ stop
7. ○ baby ○ penny ○ cherry
8. ○ snow ○ boat ○ bowl
9. ○ tray ○ blow ○ rainbow
10. ○ toad ○ toast ○ book
11. ○ tie ○ pail ○ pie
12. ○ bow ○ toe ○ train

A Book of Riddles

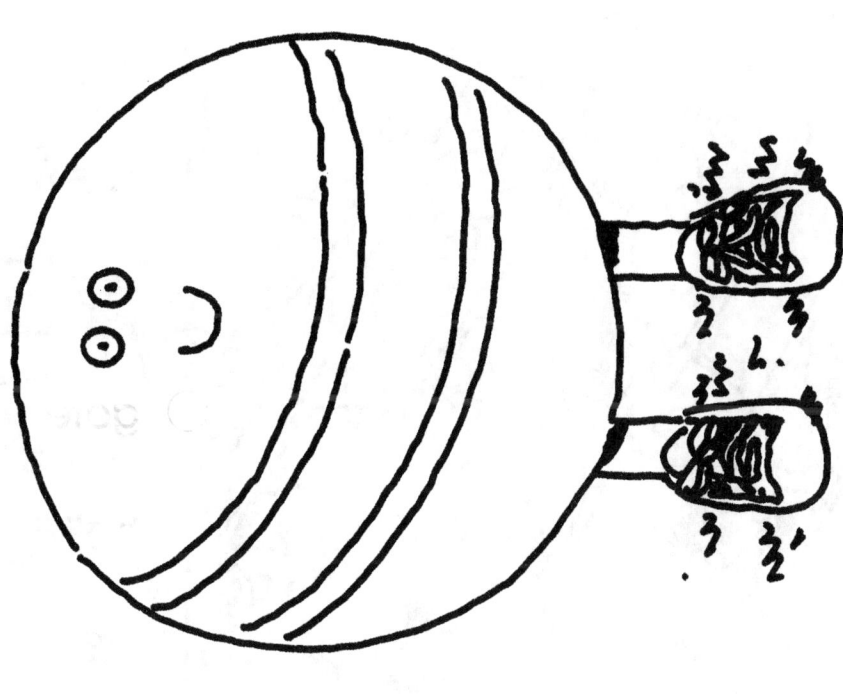

A football.

What do you call a ball that has feet?

1

A cabbage, because it is a head.

Who would win a race, a potato or a cabbage?

4

What do you call a baseball team that is asleep?

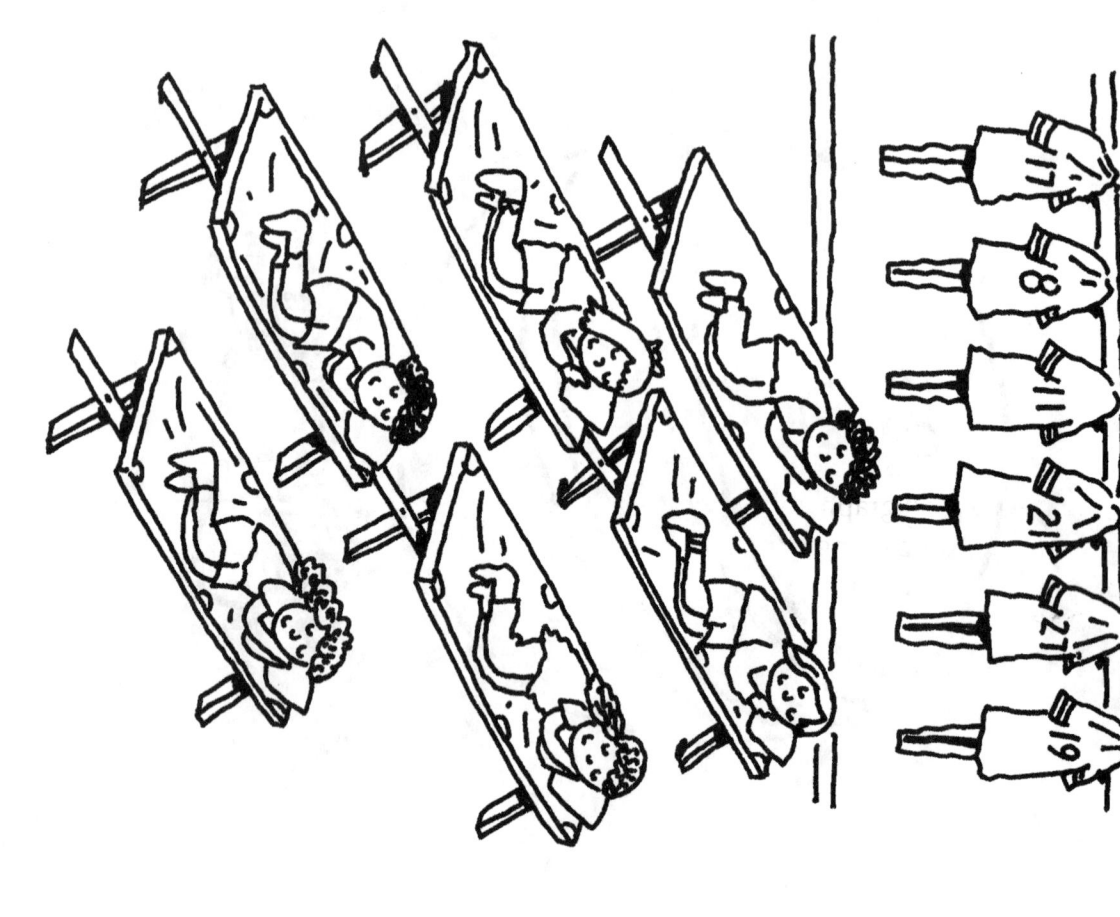

A dream team.

What do you call swimming lessons?

Pool school.

Classroom Fun

Vowel Digraphs

Digraph Hats

Arrange six children in a circle, each facing the other's back, and put a hat on the head of one child. Tell this child to take off the hat and put it on the head of the next child as you read a list of words. Ask children to listen for a word that has a certain digraph and when they hear you say it, to stop passing the hat. For example, if children are listening for a word with an *ea* digraph, as in *peach*, you might say, "boot, row, coast, sheep, mail, *jeans*." The person with the hat leaves the circle, and the game continues. When there are only two children left, they stand face to face, moving the hat back and forth quickly. The child left *not* wearing the hat is the winner.

Digraph Scavenger Hunt

Divide the class into four groups, one each for long *a*, long *e*, long *o*, and one for the long and short sounds of *oo*. Tell children they will be going on a scavenger hunt for things whose names have these vowel digraphs. Have each group first brainstorm a list of items they can look for. Then, give groups about 10 minutes to find objects in the classroom. Let the game continue throughout the day (perhaps on the playground, in the cafeteria, and so on). Have the groups "show and tell" at the end of the day.

Ring-Around-a-Digraph

To play this game with a large group, have children hold hands in two concentric rings facing one another. Put the same number of children in each ring (those in the outer ring will stretch their arms farther). Give each player a word that contains a digraph. Use exactly the same list of digraphs for both "rings" to ensure that each child will find a match. Then have the rings parade in opposite directions until you say "Stop." Each pair of adjoining children tells each other their words. If the words have the same digraph with the same pronunciation (for example, *goat/road, trail/rain, play/pay*), the two leave the ring and go to a winners' area. The game is over when everyone has "won."

Classroom Fun

Write a Funny Story

Tell children they will write a funny story using words they have learned in this book. Duplicate the Story Shapes Patterns on page 28 and fill in the word choices shown below. Then distribute the patterns to children. Without disclosing the story below, have them circle one thing from each shape. Then write this story frame on chart paper or reproduce it for children, leaving long blanks for children to fill in:

Once upon a time there was a ❶ _____ ▲2 _____. One day the ▲2 _____ looked ■3 _____. There was a ◆4 _____! "Will you be my pet?" the ▲2 _____ asked. I will feed you ★5 _____. You can sleep ◆6 _____. "Okay," said the ◆4 _____ and it came inside. And the ▲2 _____ and the ◆4 _____ are both happy to this very day.

❶
happy
sad
lucky
sleepy
small
tall

▲2
queen
baby
cook
football team
man named Mr. Clay

■3
out on the back lawn
on a train
in the woods
in a pail
in a haystack

◆4
monkey
bunny
puppy
snail
seal
sheep

★5
cherry pie and steak
bread and cream
wheat toast and jam
a bowl of green beans

◆6
in a tree
in a haystack
in the bedroom
at the zoo
at school

Children will enjoy illustrating their stories. Have children take turns reading their stories to their classmates from an "author's chair" and sharing their illustrations. Use the story shapes patterns again with new lists of words as your class goes on to other phonics elements.

Words in a Box

On index cards, write about ten one-syllable words with vowel digraphs, and cut them in two. The first part should be the beginning consonant sound or sounds, and the second part should be the vowel and any ending sound or sounds. Put the first-part cards in one box and the second-part cards in another box. Have children take turns choosing a card from each box and putting the cards together to see if they make a word. As children make words, have them write the words in a list under their name. If the child cannot make a word, the next child takes a turn. Keep returning cards to the appropriate box after each turn. The child with the longest list wins.

Make a Word Chain

Challenge children to make a word chain that is as long as possible within a certain time limit. Begin the chain by writing a word such as *seat* on the chalkboard. Invite children to change one letter at a time to make a new word. They can exchange a letter, drop a letter, or add a letter. For example, you might have a chain that looks like this:

*s*eat, **m**e*at*, m*eal*, **s**ea*l*, sea**m**, **s**team, *team*, **b**eam

Have children work in teams. Give one point for each word the team makes and two points for each word that has a vowel digraph.

Word and Picture Card Sort

Invite small groups of children to use the Word Cards and Picture Cards on pages 30–31 for sorting. First, have children sort the Picture Cards according to vowel sounds (long *a*, long *e*, long *o*, long *i*, short and long *oo*, short *e*, and the sound of *aw*). Then have them sort the Word Cards according to spelling (noting that *steak, bread,* and *leaf* have the same *ea* spelling but different vowel sounds). Encourage children to come up with other ways to sort the cards, such as by beginning sounds, ending sounds, and so on.

Riddle Fun

Write words with vowel digraphs on small slips of paper and place the slips in a can or bag. Have children take turns choosing a word and creating riddle clues for the word. Encourage them to think of clues for word meaning as well as the way the word sounds. Have them give their hardest clue first, then an easier one, until the class guesses the word. Model the first riddle for them, pausing after each clue: "This is an animal. It is a baby horse. Its name begins with an *f*. It ends in *l*. It has the long *o* sound." *(foal)* As children try to come up with their own clues, prompt them when necessary.

Freeze Spelling

Give children large cards, some with vowel digraphs (*ea, ai, ea, ee, oa, oo, o, ow, ay, ie, all, aw, oe*), and some with consonants that stand for beginning and ending consonant sounds (*t, l, c, sp, k, d, p, t, st, m, n, cl, tr, sn, sp, sh, ch*). Have children mingle, finding out what letters and letter combinations are available. Then, say "Start!" and have children find at least two other children that have letters that make a word. When a group of children make a word, have them shout "Word!" Then have the entire class "freeze" until the group spells its word as you write it on the chalkboard. See how many words the class can make in a ten-minute period.

What Did I Say?

Many children love to find mistakes. Your class can have fun correcting intentional errors that you generate. Write sentences on the chalkboard with mistakes involving words with digraphs, and invite children to correct them. For example:

Every night you brush your *jeep*. (teeth)
Ice cream tastes *clean*. (sweet)
A king is married to a *bean*. (queen)
Dad cuts the grass on the *street*. (lawn)

Classroom Fun

Instant Activities

Silent Letters To help children see how the second letter is silent in vowel pairs like *ai, ay, ea, ee, oa, oe,* and *ie,* write words like *rain, day, bean, bee, road, toe,* and *tie* on the chalkboard. For each word, have children circle the vowel whose name can be heard and underline the silent letter.

Bean Toss Write different vowel digraphs on slips of paper and place each slip in a cup of a muffin tin. Have children take turns tossing a bean into the muffin tin. They must then say a word that has the vowel digraph written on the slip in the cup where their bean landed.

Alike or Different? Say word pairs like the ones below, one at a time, and have children raise their hands if the words have the same vowel sound: *wheel/sleep, pail/road, he/me, brain/sail, cheap/tray, blow/row, coach/float, moon/food, crook/croak.*

Make a Word Write the vowel pairs *ee, ea, oo, oa,* and *ai* in columns on chart paper or on the chalkboard. Challenge children to make as many words as they can from each digraph by adding consonants or consonant blends before or after the vowel pair.

Missing Letters Write these mystery words and have children add a vowel digraph that completes each one: sw_ _t (sweet, sweat); m_ _n (moon, mean, main); ch_ _n (chain); gr_ _(grow, gray); bl_ _(blow); j_ _p (jeep); st_ _l (steal, steel, stool); sp_ _k (speak); s_ _k (seek, soak). Have children use each word they form in a sentence.

Sound of the Day Declare each day a vowel sound day, such as Long *a* Day. Hang a large piece of paper on the wall, and have children write words or draw pictures whose names have digraphs that make the long *a* sound. At the end of the day, read aloud all the words. Repeat with long *o,* long *e,* short *oo,* long *oo,* and the sound *aw.*

Mime Me Invite children to take turns pantomiming actions for words with vowel digraphs, such as *yawn, crawl, straw, cloak, slow, rainbow, broom, shook, coach, toad, coat, sleep, greet, scream, steal, leap,* and *sneak*. Have the rest of the class guess the words.

Rhyme Time Place the Picture Cards from page 31 face down on a table or desk. Have children take turns choosing one and saying as many rhyming words as they can. Accept words with different spellings, such as *toe, go,* and *glow*.

Only Digraphs, Please! Write words with short vowels, such as *pin, red, men, cot,* and *lap* on the chalkboard. Invite children to make a new word by adding another vowel to the word, creating a digraph. *(pain, read, mean, coat, leap)*

Digraph Story Brainstorm a list of words with a particular digraph and list them on chart paper. Begin a story and have each child add one sentence to it. Tell children that each sentence must have a word with that digraph. For example, you could begin a story with digraph *ee: Once upon a time a queen lived in a castle.*

Bag Words Place the Word Cards from page 30 in a bag. Have children take turns choosing three words and using all three in a sentence. Encourage silliness. For example: *The baby ate hay out of a bowl.*

Instant Activities

Story Shapes Patterns

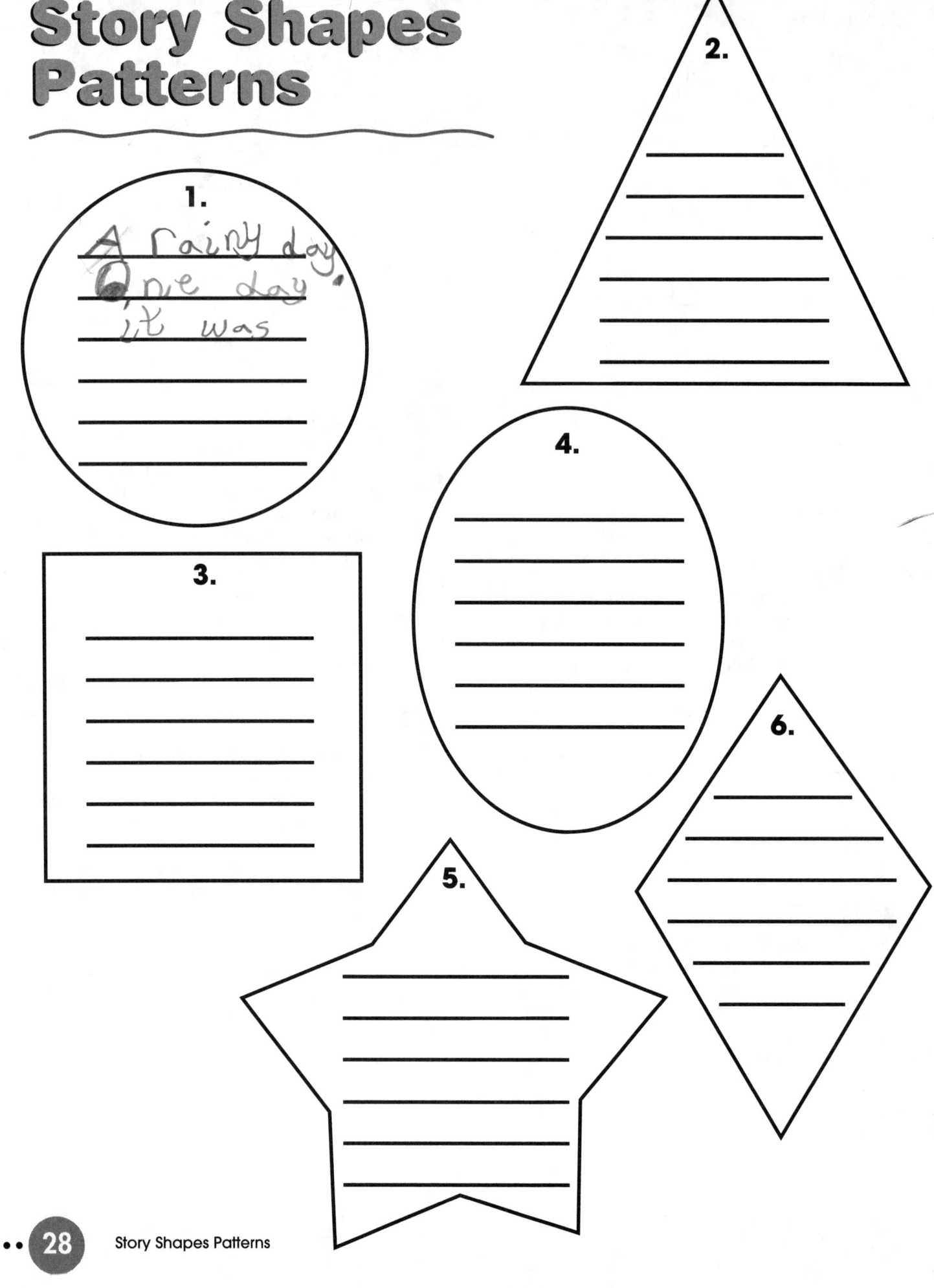

1. A rainy day, One day it was

Story Shapes Patterns

Word Bank

Below is a list of words that you may use to illustrate words with vowel digraphs. Some of these words are included in the Word/Picture Card set on pages 30–31. Ideas for using these cards and additional cards you may create yourself can be found in "Classroom Fun," pages 23–25.

Vowel Digraphs

ai	e	ea (long a)	o	oo (long)
braid	be	break	go	cool
brain	he	great	no	food
chain	me	steak	so	hoop
rain	she			shoot
train	we	**ee**	**oa**	zoo
		cheek	coach	
aw	**ea (long e)**	deep	coast	**ow**
draw	clean	screen	goal	bowl
jaw	cream	seed	soak	know
paw	meat	sheet	throat	show
saw	read			slow
straw	speak	**ey**	**oe**	snow
		key	doe	
ay	**ea (short e)**	money	hoe	**y (long e)**
day	bread	monkey	toe	funny
gray	breath	valley		happy
jay	head		**oo (short)**	lucky
pay	steady	**ie**	crook	rocky
play	sweater	fried	good	sleepy
		pie	shook	
		tie	stood	
			wool	

Teacher Notes

Page 6 See page 4, "Working with the Poem."

Page 7 *Answers:* jeans, tree, wheel, bee, jeep, sheep, meal, stream; meal.

Page 8 *Answers:* Across: 2. wheel 4. jeep 5. steam.
Down: 1. sheep (given) 3. leaf 4. jeans.

Page 9 *Answers:* 1. tray 2. clay 3. pail 4. chain. *Riddle answer:* rain.

Page 10 *Answers:* 1. toe 2. tie 3. pie 4. hoe.

Page 11 *Answers:* **blue:** feet, mean, meat, jeep, sheep, beak; **red:** tried, hoe, fried, lie, Joe, spied, doe, dried, pie, tie, toe, foe; **yellow:** day, rain, brain, gray, play, nail, main, aid, braid, jay, mail, wait.

Page 12 *Answers:* 1. go 2. elbow 3. snow 4. blow.

Page 13 *Answers:* 1. toad, road 2. coat, goat 3. boat, float.

Page 14 *Preparation:* Emphasize the long *e* sound in the second syllable, as you read aloud the words in the box to help children focus on the pictures they are looking for. *Answers:* cherry, baby, bunny, puppy, daisy, monkey, key, penny. *Riddle answer:* mon**key**.

Page 15 *Answers:* pool/school, book/hook, moon/spoon, boot/root.

Page 16 *Answers:* shook (given), look, cook, took, hook; good, wood, stood.

Page 17 *Game Directions:* Have children mix the cards and turn them face down. The first player turns two cards face up. The player says both words out loud. If the words have the same vowel sound, the player keeps them and takes another turn. If not, cards must be turned face down and the other player takes a turn. The game is over when the children have picked up all the cards.
Answers: Long *e*: leaf, peach, jeans, seal, bean.
Long *a*: steak, break.
Short *e*: bread, sweater, head, thread, feather.

Page 18 *Answers:* yawn, paw, draw, saw, straw, claw, shawl, fawn.

Page 19 *Game Directions:* Players take turns rolling a number cube, moving that number of spaces, and saying the word in the space. To stay there, the player must then say another word with the same vowel sound or return to the previous location. The first player to reach the treasure wins.

Page 20 *Answers:* Children will fill in the circle next to the appropriate word. 1. jeans 2. boot 3. sheep 4. hook 5. nail 6. sweater 7. baby 8. bowl 9. tray 10. toad 11. pie 12. toe.

Word Cards

nail	tray	leaf	tree
key	toe	tie	coat
book	pool	bowl	baby
bread	break	ball	draw